D0536046

LOOKING AT
COUNTRIES

Looking at
CARIBBEAN
Countries

Jillian Powell

PUBLISHING
A Member of the WRC Media Family of Companies

Please visit our web site at: www.garethstevens.com
For a free color catalog describing Gareth Stevens Publishing's list
of high-quality books and multimedia programs, call 1-800-542-2595 (USA)
or 1-800-387-3178 (Canada). Gareth Stevens Publishing's fax: (414) 332-3567.

Library of Congress Cataloging-in-Publication Data

Powell, Jillian.
    Looking at Caribbean countries / Jillian Powell.
      p. cm. — (Looking at countries)
    Includes index.
    ISBN-13: 978-0-8368-7667-3 (lib. bdg.)
    ISBN-13: 978-0-8368-7674-1 (softcover)
    1. Caribbean Area—Juvenile literature. I. Title.
  F2161.5.P69   2006
  972.9—dc22   2006034462

This North American edition first published in 2007 by
Gareth Stevens Publishing
A Member of the WRC Media Family of Companies
330 West Olive Street, Suite 100
Milwaukee, Wisconsin 53212 USA

This U.S. edition copyright © 2007 by Gareth Stevens, Inc.
Original edition copyright © 2006 by Franklin Watts.
First published in Great Britain in 2006 by Franklin Watts,
338 Euston Road, London NW1 3BH, United Kingdom.

Series editor: Sarah Peutrill
Art director: Jonathan Hair
Design: Rita Storey
Picture research: Diana Morris

Gareth Stevens editor: Dorothy L. Gibbs
Gareth Stevens art direction: Tammy West
Gareth Stevens graphic designer: Charlie Dahl

Photo credits: (t=top, b=bottom, l=left, r=right, c=center)
Tony Arruza/Corbis: 25b. Yann Arthus-Bertrand/Corbis: 4. Tom Bean/Corbis: 8. Richard Bickel/Corbis: 17.
Jonathan Blair/Corbis: 7. Pablo Corral V/Corbis: 25t. Howard Davies/Corbis: 16. Eye Ubiquitous/Hutchison: 18, 23.
Kevin Fletcher/Corbis: 13. Owen Franken/Corbis: 15. Stephen Frink/Corbis: 20. Philippe Giraud/Sygma/Corbis: 19t.
R. Hackenburg/zefa/Corbis: 26. Glen Hinkson/Reuters/Corbis: 9b. Jeremy Horner/Panos Pictures: 27. Dave G. Houser/
Post-Houserstock/Corbis: 19b. Jonathan Kaplan/Still Pictures: 10. Bob Krist/Corbis: 11, 14. Buddy Mays/Corbis: 22.
Gideon Mendel/Corbis: 12. Helene Rogers/Alamy: 21c. Galen Rowell/Corbis: 6. Superbild/A1 Pix: cover, 1, 9t, 21t, 24.

Contents

Where is the Caribbean?   4

The Landscape   6

Weather and Seasons   8

Caribbean People   10

School and Family   12

Country Life   14

City Life   16

Caribbean Houses   18

Caribbean Food   20

At Work   22

Having Fun   24

Caribbean Countries: The Facts   26

Glossary   28

Find Out More   29

My Map of the Caribbean   30

Index   32

Words that appear in the glossary are printed in **boldface** type the first time they occur in the text.

Where is the Caribbean?

The Caribbean is a region, or area, of the **tropics** that lies between the Atlantic Ocean and the Caribbean Sea.

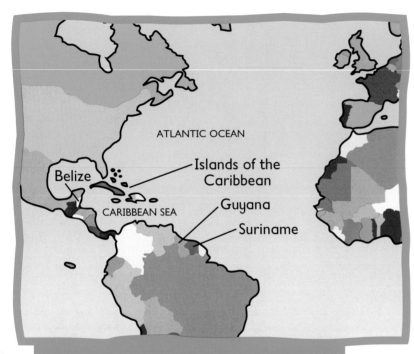

ATLANTIC OCEAN

Islands of the Caribbean

Belize

CARIBBEAN SEA

Guyana

Suriname

The region known as "the Caribbean" gets its name from the Caribbean Sea.

It includes more than seven thousand islands, as well as the mainland countries of Belize, Guyana, and Suriname.

Caribbean islands range in size from Cuba, which is the largest island of the Greater Antilles, to the smaller islands of the Bahamas and the Lesser Antilles.

This view from the air shows several small islands of the Lesser Antilles.

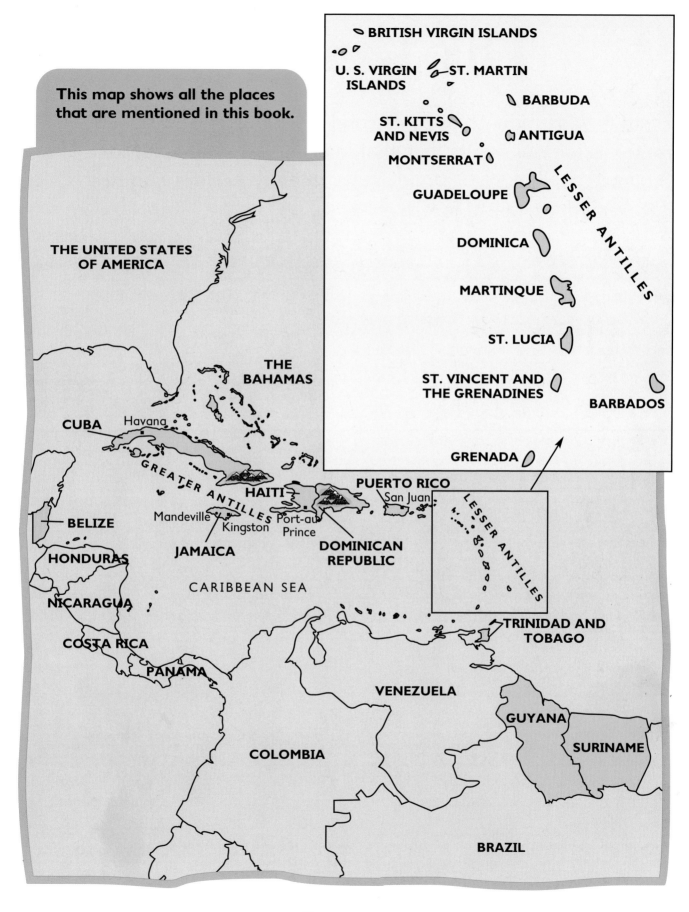

This map shows all the places that are mentioned in this book.

BRITISH VIRGIN ISLANDS

U. S. VIRGIN ISLANDS ST. MARTIN

BARBUDA

ST. KITTS AND NEVIS ANTIGUA

MONTSERRAT

GUADELOUPE

LESSER ANTILLES

DOMINICA

MARTINQUE

ST. LUCIA

ST. VINCENT AND THE GRENADINES

BARBADOS

GRENADA

THE UNITED STATES OF AMERICA

THE BAHAMAS

CUBA

Havana

GREATER ANTILLES

HAITI

PUERTO RICO

San Juan

BELIZE

Mandeville

Kingston

Port-au-Prince

LESSER ANTILLES

HONDURAS

JAMAICA

DOMINICAN REPUBLIC

NICARAGUA

CARIBBEAN SEA

TRINIDAD AND TOBAGO

COSTA RICA

PANAMA

VENEZUELA

GUYANA

SURINAME

COLOMBIA

BRAZIL

The Landscape

From its high mountains to its sandy beaches, the Caribbean region is famous for its beautiful landscapes. The mountains on many of the larger islands have steep waterfalls and are covered with tropical forests.

The island of St. Lucia has many tall mountains.

Barbados is a flat island with gentle hills.

Some of the smaller islands, such as Barbados and Antigua, have low, flat landscapes. Other islands have **salt marshes** or swampy areas where **mangrove trees** grow.

The islands of the Caribbean are surrounded by warm tropical seas. Many have bays with **coral reefs** and white-sand beaches.

Did you know?

The beaches of Harbour Island, in the Bahamas, have pink sand.

Weather and Seasons

The Caribbean has a tropical climate, which means it has plenty of hot sunshine and a lot of rain. The weather is warm all year, with cooling winds blowing in from the Atlantic Ocean.

During the dry season, from December through May, the weather is very warm, with a few rain showers.

This tropical rain forest on the island of Puerto Rico is called El Yunque. It is the Caribbean National Forest.

The warm weather and beautiful beaches attract tourists to the Dominican Republic and other Caribbean islands.

The wet season, from June through November, has heavy rains and flooding. Between July and October, the rain storms are sometimes hurricanes. The winds in hurricanes blow up to 185 miles (300 kilometers) per hour. They destroy buildings and crops and blow down power lines.

Hurricanes can destroy whole cities and towns. This hurricane damage is in Grenada.

Did you know?

The hurricanes each year are given names. The first letters of the names follow the order of the alphabet.

Caribbean People

The people of the Caribbean are a mix of many races and **cultures**, especially from Europe, Africa, and Asia. Only a few have Arawak or Carib **ancestors**. The Arawaks and Caribs are the **Amerindian** peoples who first settled in the Caribbean region.

Spanish, English, Dutch, and French are some of the many languages spoken in Caribbean countries. Some Caribbean people speak **Patois** or **Creole**. These local languages are a mix of English and European or African languages.

This man in Guyana works as a logger. His ancestors were Amerindian people.

These people in the British Virgin Islands are leaving a Christian church service.

Many people in Caribbean countries are Christians. Some are Muslims, Hindus, or **Rastafarians**, and some practice African religions that worship their own special gods or worship ancestors.

School and Family

Most children in Caribbean countries start going to school when they are five years old. They go to secondary school, or high school, from about age eleven to age fifteen. After that, some continue going to school, while others train for jobs or start working at a job.

These children from Haiti go to a school on a plantation in the Dominican Republic because their parents work there.

These boys are playing baseball on a back street in Trinidad.

Many families in Caribbean countries do not have a lot of money, and the children from poor families do not have many clothes or toys. They often make up their own games, sometimes using bats and balls and other toys they make themselves.

The poorest children are the street children of Haiti. Some are **orphans** and have no homes, schooling, or health care. Charities try to take care of these children.

Country Life

In the Bahamas, women often carry their goods on their heads when they go to markets.

People living in country towns and villages often have small plots of land where they grow vegetables or keep animals such as goats.

Sometimes, women from the villages take their vegetables to markets and sell them to get money. Fruits and vegetables are also sold at stalls, or stands, along country roads.

On Caribbean beaches, people often sell fish, fresh from the fishing boats.

On this plantation in Martinique, sugar cane is harvested by machine.

Country people in the Caribbean also find work on sugar cane, banana, or coffee plantations. Although farm machinery is now used on many plantations, some of the crops are still picked by hand.

Did you know?

The vegetables and fruits grown on Caribbean plantations are sold all over the world.

City Life

About three-quarters of the Caribbean people live in cities. The busiest places with the most people are the capital cities, including Kingston, in Jamaica; Havana, in Cuba; and Port-au-Prince, in Haiti.

The business district in Jamaica's capital city, Kingston, has many tall office buildings.

The capital cities of Caribbean countries have grown quickly. These cities have many high-rise buildings that contain banks, offices, shops, and museums.

To go places in Port-au-Prince, many people ride on brightly painted buses like this one.

City streets in Caribbean countries are crowded with buses, trucks, taxis, and bicycles. Vehicles such as tap-tap buses in Haiti and coco taxis in Havana are often painted bright colors.

Caribbean Houses

There are many different styles of houses in Caribbean countries.

Many people live in apartment buildings in the **suburbs**. The richest people live in their own individual houses. Their houses often have gardens and modern features, such as satellite television and air-conditioning.

These girls are walking home from school in Havana, Cuba. They live in large, city apartment buildings.

The poorest people in Caribbean cities live on the outskirts, or border areas, usually in crowded shantytowns. Their houses, or shanties, are made from scraps of tin and wood and have no electricity or running water.

A typical Caribbean house is made of wood and painted in bright colors.

These wooden houses in Barbados were built so they could be taken apart and rebuilt when families had to move to find work.

In country areas of the Caribbean, most houses are one-story **bungalows** made of wood, with tin or palm-**thatch** roofs. Many have covered porches, or **verandas**. Most of the windows have shutters that can be closed to keep the house cool inside.

Did you know?

The country town of Mandeville, in Jamaica, has English-style cottages built around a village green.

Caribbean Food

The foods of the Caribbean combine many styles of cooking, including European, African, and Asian, as well as Arawak and Carib. "Jerk pork" is a well-known Arawak dish from Jamaica. It is spiced pork cooked on a barbecue grill. Spices are very important in Caribbean cooking. Many Caribbean dishes combine tropical fruits with meat or salted fish.

"Fast food" in the Caribbean often means food cooked, on the spot, in street stalls, like this one in Puerto Rico.

This open-air banana market in St. Martin is right on the beach!

This supermarket in St. Lucia offers a wide choice of fruits and vegetables.

Other popular Caribbean dishes include rice and peas cooked in coconut milk and soups or stews made with salted fish and root vegetables. Both outdoor markets and supermarkets sell a variety of fruits, including mangoes and bananas, and root vegetables, such as **cassava**, potatoes, and yams.

Did you know?

Grenada is called the "isle of spices." Nutmeg is even pictured on the country's flag.

At Work

In Caribbean cities, people find jobs in offices, shops, schools, and banks. Caribbean people work in food processing and textile factories, too. Cities with large seaports may also have factories for refining oil or making cement.

Because Caribbean countries attract so many tourists, many people, especially on the islands, have jobs on cruise ships or in hotels or restaurants.

This St. Martin factory is an oil refinery and desalination plant.

This worker's job is packing bananas at a food processing plant on St. Lucia.

Outside the cities, many Caribbean people earn money by farming or fishing. Some work for big foreign companies, cutting down trees or planting and harvesting crops on sugar or banana plantations. Near the coasts, people harvest food products such as sea moss and sea urchins.

Did you know?

The Caribbean is the world's most popular area for travel on cruise ships.

Having Fun

The people of the Caribbean love festivals, music, and dancing. At Carnival time, they dress up in colorful costumes and parade, on foot or on floats, through city streets.

For children in Antigua, _Carnival_ means "fun"!

The instruments in a steel band look like big metal pans.

Steel bands, **calypso**, and **reggae** are all styles of music from Caribbean countries. In countries such as Puerto Rico and Cuba, people dance in clubs, at parties, and even on the streets.

Sports are also popular activities. Caribbean people enjoy watching basketball, **cricket**, and football games. In the warm Caribbean weather, children love to play outdoor games such as street tennis or beach cricket.

This beach in Barbados is a good place for a game of beach cricket.

Caribbean Countries: The Facts

- The Caribbean is made up of thirty-two different countries. Fifteen of the countries are full members of the Caribbean Community and Common Market (CARICOM). The Caribbean region also includes the Spanish-speaking states of Cuba and the Dominican Republic, along with territories that belong to Britain, France, the Netherlands, or the United States.

- The Caribbean region has three main groups of islands: the Bahamas, the Greater Antilles, and the Lesser Antilles. The largest islands are in the Greater Antilles.

Each country in the Caribbean has its own flag. This flag is for Cuba.

Havana, Cuba, is the largest capital city in the Caribbean countries. More than two million people live in Havana.

- The main currencies, or kinds of money, used in Caribbean countries include the East Caribbean dollar, the United States dollar, and the euro. In Spanish-speaking Cuba and the Dominican Republic, the main currency is the peso.

Did you know?

The Caribbean Sea was named after the Caribs, who were among the earliest settlers on the islands.

Glossary

Amerindians – the original native peoples of South America

ancestors – family members who lived in the past

bungalows – small, one-story houses, usually with a porch

calypso – lively music from the West Indies, often with songs that tell funny stories

cassava – a tropical plant with a starchy root that is used to thicken liquid foods

coral reefs – mounds or ridges of coral rising out of the seabed

Creole – a mixture of the English and French languages

cricket – a popular British team sport played with bats and balls, but the game is not like baseball

cultures – the ways and beliefs of certain civilizations, nationalities, societies, or other large groups of people

desalination – the process of removing salt from seawater

mangrove trees – tropical trees that grow in saltwater along seacoasts and have stiltlike roots growing out of their branches

orphans – children who do not have any living parents

Patois – a local English dialect spoken by Jamaican-born blacks

plantation – a large farm that grows crops such as coffee and bananas to sell to both home and foreign markets

Rastafarians – people who follow Rastafarianism, a religion started by black Jamaicans

reggae – a style of music that mixes native Jamaican rhythms with rock and soul

salt marshes – low-lying wetlands near the sea

suburbs – the areas that surround a large city, where people who work in the city often have their homes

thatch – plant material, such as grass, straw, or branches, used as a protective covering

tropics – the warm, wet regions of Earth that lie close to the equator

verandas – covered porches or open areas along the fronts or sides of houses

Find Out More

Boricua Kids (History of Puerto Rico for Children)
www.elboricua.com/BoricuaKids.html

Caribbean National Forest Kids Page
www.fs.fed.us/r8/caribbean/kids-page/

Eye on the Caribbean
www.globaleye.org.uk/primary_autumn04/eyeon/intro.html

Talk Jamaican!
www.jamaicans.com/speakja/talk.htm

Publisher's note to educators and parents: Our editors have carefully reviewed these Web sites to ensure that they are suitable for children. Many Web sites change frequently, however, and we cannot guarantee that a site's future contents will continue to meet our high standards of quality and educational value. Be advised that children should be closely supervised whenever they access the Internet.

My Map of the Caribbean

Photocopy or trace the map on page 31. Then write in the names of the island groups, bodies of water, countries, and capital cities listed below. (Look at the map on page 5 if you need help.)

After you have written in the names of all the places, find some crayons and color the map!

Island Groups

Bahamas
British Virgin Islands
Greater Antilles
Lesser Antilles
U.S. Virgin Islands

Bodies of Water

Atlantic Ocean
Caribbean Sea

Mainland Countries

Belize
Guyana
Suriname

Capital Cities

Havana
Kingston
Port-au-Prince
San Juan

Island Countries

Antigua and Barbuda
Barbados
Cuba
Dominica
Dominican Republic
Grenada
Guadeloupe
Haiti
Jamaica
Martinique
Puerto Rico
St. Kitts and Nevis
St. Lucia
St. Martin
St. Vincent and the Grenadines
Trinidad and Tobago

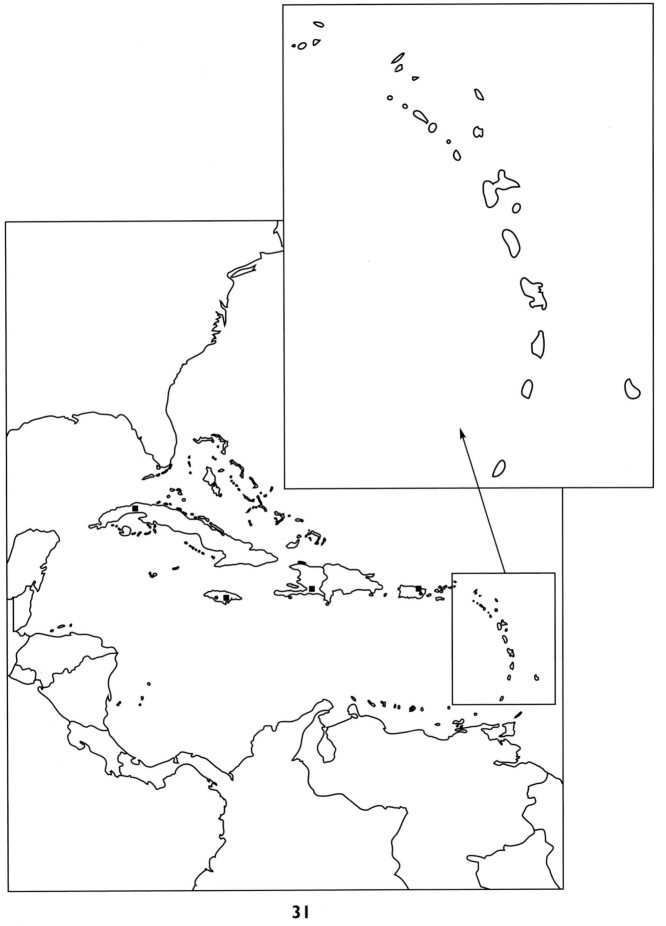

Index

Amerindians 10
Antigua 5, 7, 24
Atlantic Ocean 4, 8

Bahamas 4, 5, 7,
    14, 26
Barbados 5, 7,
    19, 25
Barbuda 5
beaches 6, 7, 9,
    14, 21, 25
Belize 4, 5

Caribbean Sea 4, 5
children 12, 13, 25
cities 16–17, 18,
    22, 23, 24, 27
country life 14–15
Cuba 4, 5, 16, 18,
    25, 26, 27

Dominica 5
Dominican Republic
    5, 9, 12, 26, 27

families 12, 13, 19
farming 15, 23

festivals 24
fishing 14, 23
flags 21, 26
foods 20–21, 22, 23

Greater Antilles 4,
    5, 26
Grenada 5, 9, 21
Guadeloupe 5
Guyana 4, 5, 10

Haiti 5, 12, 13, 17
houses 18–19
hurricanes 9

Jamaica 5, 11, 16,
    19, 20
jobs 12, 22–23

languages 10
Lesser Antilles 4,
    5, 26

Martinique 5, 15
money 27
mountains 6
music 24, 25, 29

plantations 12,
    15, 23
Puerto Rico 5, 8,
    20, 25

rain 8, 9
religions 11

schools 12, 13, 22
sports 25
St. Kitts and
    Nevis 5
St. Lucia 5, 6, 21, 23
St. Martin 5, 21, 22
St. Vincent and the
    Grenadines 5
Suriname 4, 5

Tobago 5
tourists 9, 22
Trinidad 5, 13, 25

Virgin Islands 5, 11

weather 8–9, 25
working 15, 22–23